DISCOVERY-BASED

RETAIL

Published
2012
By
Discovery-Based Retail
© 2012 Philip H. Mitchell & Gary A. Petz

(888) 292-6531

Publisher's Note

Disclaimer

Rockin' Retail Lessons

Volume 1

By

Philip H. Mitchell

And

Gary Petz

Discovery-Based Retail

Contents

Introduction

Driving home one day after presenting a seminar to a group of retailers Gary and I were reviewing how the day had gone. We were pleased!

He was driving and I was in charge of the radio so I found a station whose format included 60's and 70's music. To most people, including Gary, these are the oldest of the oldies. To me, it's just great music. I have eclectic tastes.

We're driving along and an old Bee Gees offering came on. "I've just got to get a message to you!"

"What a great theme for a retail lesson!" Gary said.

"Yes it is." I replied, without really thinking about it that much.

As we drove further, however, Jim Croce began to croon "Like the pine trees lining the winding road, I've got a name, I've got a name." Instantly I began to understand what Gary was already thinking. Within the title of this song was another great retail lesson.

The problem with simple retail lessons is that they can be boring. What if we could "spice them up" a little bit? What if we had a series of really short reminder lessons inspired by song titles?

It would make for good reading when time was short. The resource might also make great discussion starters for store meetings. The organizer could play the song that inspired the upcoming message and ask the participants to guess what the meeting was to be about. Who knows? They might guess something entirely different and possibly even more "on point". At the very least it would be a departure from the routine to which many retail staff meetings decay.

This is the first of what we intend to be several books in this series. Our promise to you is that the messages will be short and informative.

We'll start with a song by the Beatles, "Paperback Writer". It is not a retail lesson, but rather a further explanation of why we spent time writing this book.

Enjoy!

Paperback Writer

From Wikipedia

*"**Paperback Writer**" is a 1966 song recorded and released by The Beatles. Written by Paul McCartney and John Lennon[4] (credited to Lennon–McCartney), the song was released as the A-side of their eleventh single. The single went to the number one spot in the United States, United Kingdom, Ireland, West Germany, Australia, New Zealand and Norway. On the US Billboard Hot 100, the song was at number one for two non-consecutive weeks, being interrupted by Frank Sinatra's "Strangers in the Night".*

"Paperback Writer" was the last new song by the Beatles to be featured on their final tour in 1966, and was the group's only U.S. number one released that year.

What moves a person to write a book? Have you ever wondered? I certainly can't speak for others. Heck, I can't even speak for Gary and he's co-writing this one. I can only tell you why I write. I love it! That's it, plain and simple. I don't expect anyone will say that I'm a particularly good writer...doesn't matter. I feel most fulfilled when I'm creating something and this book is a creation. You will have to judge for yourself whether it's worthwhile or not. And, from my perspective, that doesn't make a lot of difference either. I still feel driven or compelled to write. I think that the creative process is a gift from God... an extension of the creative process that is our genesis and our genius. There you go: that's the "why" in a nutshell. And that's about all I've got to say about that.

Mitchell and Petz

When we wrote Discovery-Based Retail and Ten Weeks to a Better Retail Operation, they were long and arduous processes. I vow from this first page that writing this book is going to be neither long nor arduous. This book is going to be fun. Fun to write and with any amount of luck, it's going to be fun to read.

The concept is simple. Gary and I have spent our working lives in retail and we want to share some of what we've learned. I don't suppose that anything we'll write will cause lightning bolts to suddenly strike your mind. (And if they do, I pray we can't be held liable.) What we do hope comes from its reading is that you will become more informed or perhaps refocused, rededicated. And maybe if your fire is ebbing you may experience some rekindling.

Retail is a business of passion. For some, recent economic times have made it difficult to stay passionate. Today, (I promise you it was today as I write this) an experienced retail manager told us that he thought many young people looked to more exciting careers, computers and the like. His eyes twinkled as he talked about retail being an honorable career that was people centered and relationship fired. It was easy to see that his flame still glowed.

No lesson will be long, but rather concise and to a specific point; some will be elementary and others more complex. The book will be arranged in no particular order. Perhaps not every lesson will be applicable to your unique situation, but I promise some will.

You will see that they have all been inspired by song titles and not coincidently older ones, a testament to the spattering of gray that now covers my temples. The one great thing about aging is that those of us fortunate enough to still be breathing are growing older together. So while you too are aging you might as well pour yourself a cup of coffee and read a couple of pages.

Magic carpet ride.

Excerpt from Wikipedia

*"**Magic Carpet Ride**" is a rock song written by <u>John Kay</u> and <u>Rushton Moreve</u> from the <u>Canadian</u>-<u>American</u> <u>hard rock</u> band <u>Steppenwolf</u>. The song was initially released in 1968 on the album <u>The Second</u>. It was the lead single from that album, peaking at No. 3 in the US, and becoming the band's second-biggest hit, surpassed only by "<u>Born to Be Wild</u>". The song is also considered the first modern rock video.*

One of the best ways to drive sales is with special events. I characterize a special event as something out of the ordinary...something to see, something to hear, something to learn or something to do. You may fall short of being able to offer Magic Carpet Rides as a promotion (although I bet that would attract a bunch of people) you can use your creativity to plan events that will draw traffic, spawn excitement and increase sales.

Don't listen to the munchkin sitting on your shoulder whispering in your ear about how much trouble special events are. Yes, they do require some planning and execution, but remember you're trying to differentiate your business, and special events are a great way to do that. I said it was a great way to drive sales, not an easy one.

Depending on what you have in mind, special events will often mean engaging the service of a specialist. You may have staff that can handle presentations, but you may be well served, instead, to announce the appearance of an outside expert. There's just something different about the way the presentation will be perceived.

Examples? OK, let's try a few. Let's say that yours is a home improvement store offering floor coverings and building products. How about bringing an expert in on Saturday to offer lessons teaching attendees how to install ceramic tile on floors and backsplashes? In this case, of course, you would want to offer the products and tools (either for sale or rent) that would empower the participants to implement what they learn.

Here's another. Let's say you're a lawn and garden store. How about lessons on building flowerbeds, water gardens or some specialty instruction like "getting started with bonsai"? A secret for your success will be tying the event to products that you sell. That should go without saying and fall into the "no-brainer" category, but I just wanted to make sure that you contrast an actual sales event promotion against a free hot dog day.

No doubt, within you organization someone has been placed in charge of marketing. As owner or manager, if your business is small, that might well be you. As you plan your promotional efforts, make sure to schedule on your calendar regular special promotions. Shoppers gravitate to activity; don't let your business be a sleepy sister. Wake her up! You never know; maybe the special events will even reenergize you and your staff.

25 or 6 to 4.

Excerpt from Wikipedia

*"**25 or 6 to 4**" is a song written by <u>American</u> musician <u>Robert Lamm</u>, one of the founding members of the <u>rock</u>/<u>jazz fusion</u> band <u>Chicago</u>. It was <u>recorded</u> for their second <u>album</u>, <u>Chicago</u> (1970), with <u>Peter Cetera</u> on lead vocals. The song was edited and released as a single in June of that year, climbing to number 4 on the U.S. <u>Billboard Hot 100</u> chart[1] and number seven on the <u>UK Singles Chart</u>. This recording features an <u>electric guitar</u> solo using a <u>wah-wah pedal</u> by Chicago guitarist <u>Terry Kath</u>, and has been included in numerous Chicago <u>compilation albums</u>.*

An updated version of "25 or 6 to 4" was recorded for the 1986 album <u>Chicago 18</u> with <u>James Pankow</u> listed as co-writer. Featuring new band member <u>Jason Scheff</u> on lead vocals, the single reached number 48 on the U.S. chart. This version was also used as the B-side for the band's next single in 1986 "<u>Will You Still Love Me?</u>".

How long has it been since you've considered your store's operating hours to determine whether you are maximizing your customer opportunities? Many store managers get entrenched in doing things the way they've always done them. Let's face it: opening and closing the store are tasks which are about as repetitive as anything one can think of. Therefore, once in place, hours of operation are rarely considered or modified.

Taking an occasional look at hours does not necessarily mean that you will decide to change anything. It does require that you focus on two very important elements: viewing your store through your customers' eyes and profitability. I think almost everybody would agree that both of those considerations would be worthwhile examinations.

Determining your store's slotting in the market place (see Discovery-Based Retail Chapter 9) can go a long way in helping you understand why your store's hours of operation can and must be different from various types of competitors even within your sales category. Compare a locally owned lumberyard or home center's hours of operation against that of a Lowe's or Home Depot, for example, and you can readily see the differences.

Likely, after you conduct this review, if you change things at all, you won't be adding or subtracting hours per day or days per week, but rather, perhaps 30 minutes in the morning or 30 minutes or an hour in the evening. If your point of sale system offers time coding of transactions this process will be fairly straightforward. You can simply review sales during the first 30 minutes of the day and last 30 minutes of the day. If the register is ringing regularly during those periods, it might be worth considering "extending" them. If your registers do not offer this capability, then old-fashioned observation will be required.

There are a couple of other things to consider. If either of those two periods is slower than you would expect or slower than other periods of the day, it might lead you to conclude that the store's bottom line might benefit from shortening hours slightly. This would have to be determined on a store-by-store level, but remember if your staff is operating at the level that they should be, there are beneficial tasks that are being accomplished during these periods too. Though the dollar value of those actions are difficult to quantify, it is certain that time is required for tasks beyond the actual sales process.

I constantly reinforce viewing your store through its customers' eyes. In fact, perhaps some who have read my books, blogs or other articles might even say that I get carried away with this point. But it seems to me that there is nothing to manage in retail if sales do not first occur. Knowing that retail sales are directly proportional to how your store appeals to its customers just seems so fundamental in the managerial process. When you examine your store in this manner, hours of operation will definitely have to be a consideration.

Mitchell and Petz

Come together.

*"**Come Together**" is a song by <u>The Beatles</u> written by <u>John Lennon</u>[1] and credited to <u>Lennon–McCartney</u>. The song is the opening track on the album <u>Abbey Road</u>, and was released as a <u>double A-sided</u> single with "<u>Something</u>", their twenty-first single in the United Kingdom and twenty-sixth in the United States. The song reached the top of the charts in the US,[2] and peaked at number four in the UK.[3]*

If currently you're not having regular store meetings, you should be. Store meetings are a great venue to exchange ideas and keep your team focused on your branding message. They present opportunities to foster teamwork, educate and spread your vision for improved operations.

I had a manager tell me recently that when he heard me recommend regular store meetings at one of our seminars he hesitantly started the process. He was elated over the change he had seen in productivity...he was surprised. He shouldn't have been. Store meetings are no more than communication. They force you as presenter or organizer to plan an agenda. When you plan an agenda it forces you to analyze problems and contemplate opportunities. Planning's a good thing...so store meetings will make you a better manager.

Nothing says that you have to be the presenter during the entire meeting. Actually the meetings will probably be more effective if you spread out that responsibility. Think about it. If in contemplation of planning an agenda it forces you to look at problems and contemplate opportunities, doesn't it stand to reason that it will do the same for the others you choose to involve?

A word of caution: don't allow meetings to turn into bitch sessions. Make it clear from the onset that while you want to hear suggestions for improvement you want the meetings to stay positive and future focused. Keep the meetings concise and limit their time. Schedule them regularly at intervals that make sense. Try to pick a time that is convenient for most involved.

One last thought. We often consult with retail operations whose employees seem to have no common vision for branding and message. Coincidently, we find that most of these stores do not conduct regular store meetings. If everybody knows where you're trying to go, they can help you get there. If, however, you have no clear vision of your store, its message and the way it fits into the retail arena within which you operate, well then, that's another problem entirely.   Get your thoughts organized and come together.

With a little help from my friends.

Excerpt from Wikipedia

*"**With a Little Help from My Friends**" (originally titled "A Little Help from My Friends") is a song written by John Lennon and Paul McCartney, released on The Beatles album Sgt. Pepper's Lonely Hearts Club Band in 1967. The song was written for and sung by The Beatles' drummer Ringo Starr as the character "Billy Shears"; it is ranked No. 304 on Rolling Stone's list of the 500 Greatest Songs of All Time.*

_____

Sometimes retail management is a lonely position. You're responsible for the realities of sales, margin, payroll, personnel...and the list goes on and on. If your store is part of a multi-store operation, that loneliness is minimized to a degree. But if you're flying solo there's a chance that you know the alone feelings that I just described. The aloneness of owning and operating a single store can put you at a disadvantage.

I always encourage storeowners to attend trade shows and seminars that foster sharing. I know...I know you don't want to share methodology and private information with local competitors and I don't blame you. But really, if your store is in Tallahassee and you meet somebody who runs a similar style operation in Phoenix what can it hurt? I've seen some wonderful long-term relationships built in just this way. One thing you can bet, the problems and issues you're facing are not new and probably not unusual.

Mitchell and Petz

Some trade organizations sponsor round table meetings. Round table meetings are meetings of storeowners and/or managers. During these meetings, information and "best practices" are shared and discussed. If you are lucky enough to avoid the meeting where one guy knows everything, these too can be helpful. Unfortunately some round table meetings get a little pricey, but I have had retailers tell me they thought the money paid dividends. It would be worth looking into.

One last thought and if this sounds blatantly like an advertisement, oh well. There are very skilled consultants who can be really helpful. The consultant tag conjures bad images in a lot of retailers' minds. I agree that there are bad, greedy and overpriced consultants just like there are bad, greedy and overpriced retailers.

The point is if you feel like you would benefit from some advice, there are sources for that advice. Seek it out!

Sounds of silence.

Excerpt from Wikipedia

*"**The Sound of Silence**" is the song that propelled the 1960s <u>folk music</u> duo <u>Simon & Garfunkel</u> to popularity. It was written in February 1964 by <u>Paul Simon</u> in the aftermath of the 1963 assassination of <u>John F. Kennedy</u>.[1] An initial version preferred by the band was remixed and <u>sweetened</u>, and has become known as "the quintessential folk rock release".[2] In the U.S., it was the duo's second most popular hit after "<u>Bridge Over Troubled Water</u>".*

Sometime silence is required, at a funeral for instance. Sometimes silence is desirable, like during a movie or at an intimate restaurant. But in a retail environment, silence makes for an uncomfortable shopping experience. So come on, crank some tunes baby and get started rocking and rolling to higher sales.

The reasons are simple. Music is entertaining and therefore it compresses the perception of shopping time. Compress perceived shopping time and customers are likely to continue shopping longer. Foster an atmosphere in which customers shop longer and you will most certainly benefit by higher sales numbers.

But here's a critical issue. You must determine what music you should play by profiling the age of your ideal customer. Your ideal customers are the ones that you consider when picking which products you are going to sell aren't they? If not they should be.

Mitchell and Petz

In fact every decision that you make regarding product and presentation should be done with this "ideal group" in mind. Otherwise, like I wrote in Discovery-Based Retail it's something akin to baiting a trap without knowing what you're trying to capture.

But anyway back to the music. Once you have decided what group you are trying to appeal to you will know instantly what music you should play. For example, people my age, mid 50s, seventies music is a good bet. Hey, if I'm in a store grooving to some Buckinghams or Grass Roots or Stones, or well, you get the picture: I'm going to take my time. I'm going to spend more money.

In addition, the age of your targeted demographic will guide you as to volume level as well. Just walk by one of the stores in a mall targeting teens and hear, or more likely feel, how they're trying to entice their target customers. Like a said, silence is a great thing in some places, but it's not appropriate for a retail environment.

Time in a bottle.

Excerpt from Wikipedia

"Time in a Bottle" *is a posthumous* <u>Billboard Hot 100</u> *and* <u>Cash Box</u> *Top 100 Singles chart number-one hit for* <u>singer-songwriter Jim Croce</u>. *The song reached the top spot on the Billboard chart at the end of December 1973, three months after his death in a plane crash. It was the third posthumous number one single on the Hot 100. At the same time, it was a number-one hit on the Billboard* <u>Easy Listening</u> *chart.*[1]

The song was originally written for Croce's son, <u>A.J.</u>,[2] *and appeared on his third album in 1972,* <u>You Don't Mess Around with Jim</u>. *The following year Croce would shoot to fame with his hit single "*<u>Bad Bad Leroy Brown</u>*", just months before the September 20 plane crash. Time in a Bottle was later used as the title for a* <u>compilation album</u> *of Croce's love songs.*

I've got a real problem! There are only 24 hours in my day and it seems that I never get everything done. Do you suffer from the same affliction? Well if so, I guess that we both need to focus on prioritizing, don't we?

As a store manager you're faced with an additional dilemma. It's not only your time and work load that you have to prioritize and manage, but your employees' as well. Here's a simple tip: Make sure that you are afforded planning time each day.

Often store managers are faced with problems and unexpected tasks from the moment they enter the store. In a "bullets are flying" environment, planning is often forgotten. Without planning, an unproductive cycle of management by reaction occurs. In fact, in that scenario the manager, as captain of the ship, is no longer piloting but rather simply hanging on.

Prioritizing is not really a difficult task. It is basically a matter of asking oneself which of two tasks is most important as regards the particular day. So, decide between two, repeat the step as many times as necessary and soon you will find that you have a prioritized list of "to dos" for the day. The problem is that planning has to be longer term than just the current day. It's important to develop a list of longer-term goals compiling a list of the intermediate steps that will be required to lead to the eventual desired result. Once you have those steps clearly outlined, blend the management of those steps into your daily scheduled planning.

The thing about time management is that it is so easy in theory. Unfortunately it is not as easily implemented. There are a number of systems that are probably helpful. I have been exposed to several and I heartily recommend one outlined in a book titled *The GO System*, written by Chris Crouch and available on Amazon. GO, in this case is an acronym for "Getting Organized".

I guess the most important thing to take from this lesson is that regardless of how busy you are it is imperative that you allow for planning time. Make planning time priority number one and don't let putting out fires steal time from this most important task. Without structured planning time you simply will not be optimally effective. It may not be saving Time in a Bottle, but as far as I have learned, it's the best we can do!

What a day for a daydream.

Excerpt from Wikipedia

*"**Daydream**" is a popular song written by John Sebastian, published in 1966. The song was originally recorded that year by Sebastian's group The Lovin' Spoonful and released on their album of the same title.*

The song reached #2 on the Billboard Hot 100[1] and also #2 on the UK singles chart. The song originated with Sebastian's attempt to rewrite The Supremes' "Baby Love".[2]

I have been criticized at points in my lifetime for daydreaming. Well, I'm old enough to now know that not only is daydreaming OK, it's a great thing. For what some people may call daydreaming, I like to think of more as something like "imagineering". If you can't dream it, you certainly can't do it and it's very important to develop a grander image of your endeavors...whatever they are.

Sometimes envisioning what the future can be starts ones juices flowing and re-ignites dormant passions. How about a store manager, let's say you for instance...what is your vision of your store a year from today...what about 5 years from today? Do you have lofty aspirations? I hope so. Do you share them with your employees? I hope so.

Here's a good exercise. Sit down and write a list of things that you would like to see changed dramatically about your business one year from today. Once you have the list compiled, separate the entries and list below each one the incremental changes that would have to occur to facilitate the dramatic changes that you envision. After you have completed this process set your exercise aside for a couple of days.

When you come back to reexamine what you have listed, it is a good bet that the incremental changes that you have listed will seem like no big deal. I'm willing to bet that you will look at them and say, "Yeah, I can do that." If that is not the case, break the incremental changes down into even smaller changes, set those aside and then reexamine your document in another day or so. There is an old Chinese proverb that states: The longest journey begins with a single step." So too, the largest changes can begin with the smallest of movements.

So as I daydream about it, I guess this day really is "custom made for a day-dreamin' boy"...or girl.

Give me just a little more time.

Excerpt from Wikipedia

"Give Me Just a Little More Time" *is the debut single for* <u>Chairmen of the Board</u>, *released in 1970 (see* <u>1970 in music</u>) *through* <u>Capitol Records</u> *on* <u>Holland–Dozier–Holland</u>'s <u>Invictus Records</u> *label.*

The song was written and produced by <u>Brian Holland</u>, <u>Lamont Dozier</u>, <u>Edward Holland, Jr.</u>, *and Ron Dunbar. Because of then still pending lawsuit against Holland-Dozier-Holland from their former employers,* <u>Motown</u>, *the trio credited themselves with the pseudonym "Edythe Wayne" for this song and many other early Invictus/<u>Hot Wax</u> releases. "Give Me Just a Little More Time" features Chairmen of the Board lead singer* <u>General Johnson</u> *as the narrator, begging a lover who rejected him to reconsider and give him "just a little more time".*

The next line of this old song went something like "and our love will surely grow". Well I don't know how the guy did with his love thing, but I do know that when it comes to your credit customers giving a little more time is not a good thing.

I read somewhere recently that 4 out of 5 businesses fail in their first five years of operation. Of the ones that survive that culling, 8 out of 10 fail in the next 5 years. The main cause for failure of any startup business is undercapitalization. The reason cited next on the list of reasons for failure is poor monitoring of customer credit. Probably nobody really enjoys working accounts receivable. But remember a failure to do so can spell disaster for your enterprise.

To help you gain a handle on this pitfall, there are key financial ratios that can help you monitor your progress with collections. These numbers will come from your balance sheet.

- Average collection period (days on the books) is an indicator of how long it is taking a retailer to turn receivables in to cash.
  - Average collection period = Average Accounts Receivable ÷ (Credit Annual Sales ÷ 365)

The result of this equation will be a number that represents days. Let's look at an example. Joe's Lumber has annual credit sales of $650,000. His average accounts receivable over a calendar year is $56,000. Average accounts receivable are figured by taking month's end receivables for each month, adding them together and dividing by 12.

His credit yearly sales of $650,000 divided by 365 equals (we'll round up) 1781. This result divided by his average accounts receivable number of $56,000 equals 31.44. Therefore, on average it takes him a little over 31 days to turn his receivables into cash. It should be Joe's goal to make incremental improvements on this variable.

Average collection period is a number that needs to be compared within your specific industry and, probably even more important, to itself over time. Comparing to industry can give you a benchmark, but comparison to self will monitor improvement. Set yourself a specific goal based on your current results and commit to lowering that number.

Rockin' Retail Lessons

Extended receivables signal trouble for any merchant because his capital is eaten up. The moneys that he would otherwise reinvest in inventory are not readily available and the deficit causes problems in meeting obligations with payroll and payables.

There are always other industry guidelines and benchmarks out there. Remember when reviewing your store's performance against that of the industry that you want to EXCEED averages. Raise the bar on your own performance and maybe yours will be a business that survives well past its 10th birthday.

Mitchell and Petz

I'm your captain.

Excerpt from Wikipedia

"I'm Your Captain (Closer to Home)" *is an epic 1970 song written by* American *musician* Mark Farner *and recorded by* Grand Funk Railroad *as the closing track to their album* Closer to Home. *Ten minutes in duration, it is the band's longest studio recording. One of the group's best-known songs, it is composed as two distinct but closely related movements. Its title has been rendered in various ways across many different Grand Funk albums, including* **"I'm Your Captain"**, **"I'm Your Captain/Closer to Home"**, **"Closer to Home/I'm Your Captain"**, **"Closer to Home (I'm Your Captain)"**, *and* **"Closer to Home"**.[1]

As commander-in-chief of your retail operation you have a number of responsibilities that your employees are completely unaware of and that's as it should be. However I want to emphasize that one responsibility, the attitude that permeates the store and eventually gets labeled as part of your brand is ultimately yours.

The other day I had the pleasure of eating at a chain restaurant location that served as a perfect example of employees adopting and adapting the attitude of their leader. The manager, friendly and concerned, made his way from table to table checking on his patrons' assessment of the food quality and service. A few moments later I then observed him communicating to his staff his expectations and the standards that he wanted to achieve. It was interesting to observe the relaxed attitude with which he communicated and yet his message was not lost on one of his workers. Everybody knew he was in charge and that was easy to see. His smile and easy, genuine concern was mirrored on the face of every person working there. The food was OK, the service experience excellent. I can't say, of course, that this was the attitude that the manager brought to the restaurant every day, but it was the attitude that he commanded at this particular time on this particular day and it was working to perfection.

Just as children learn from example, so too, do employees. Set high standards and expectations by demanding the same from yourself. Customers are job one in any successful retail operation and the moment that ceases to be the case, opinion of your store and its brand deteriorates.

A friend of mine just got word this past week that his bank was no longer going to renew his operating loan. He is in no condition to continue without it. As I write this, not even his employees are aware of the store's imminent demise. I had reviewed with him his P&Ls and it became crystal clear that the store started sliding long before the economy did. What had transpired at this time, I asked. With further review it was determined that the slide started at about the same time they lost a manager to better opportunities. That manager, I am told, set an atmosphere much like the one I described in the restaurant. When he left, so did that special something that comes from making customers job one and enjoying that responsibility

As my friend expressed remorse over his operation's demise, I felt sad that he hadn't realized the situation as it developed. So here are my final thoughts; take care of your customers or some other store will and that attitude must begin with you. You are the captain.

Never can say goodbye.

Excerpt from Wikipedia:

"Never Can Say Goodbye" *is a song written by* <u>Clifton Davis</u> *and originally recorded by* <u>The Jackson 5</u>. *Released as a* <u>single</u> *in 1971, it was one of the group's most successful songs. The song has been covered numerous times, most notably in 1974 by* <u>disco</u> <u>diva</u> <u>Gloria Gaynor</u> *and in 1987 by* <u>Hi-NRG</u>/*dance-pop group* <u>The Communards</u>.

During our consults with independent hardware and home center dealers we have had the opportunity to deal with different people working with varied backgrounds and training. It often presents very interesting situations. For example we dealt with one operation in which the fundamental tenant was that no opportunity walked. Price was set as a starting point but everything was negotiable and if anything and I mean anything, could be done to prevent a "no sale", those steps were taken. The results were instant discounts and deep slashing of prices to anyone who even mildly protested price.

As you might suspect the business was doing good volume, but was it any wonder that they constantly struggled with margin? In fact, it might be suggested that they were invoking classical conditioning on their customers and simply training them to complain about prices. If people complained about prices, did it loud enough, or simply turned to walk out the prices magically changed to meet their desires. Now I admit this is an extreme example and it's the only time that we have seen this level of price caving. But the point is that there really is such a thing as bad business. In the case where a customer does not allow you to make money from the relationship it's time to fire that customer!

Of course, this is not the only circumstance that should have you examining whether or not you'd be better off without the business. If a customer is constantly complaining about your products, prices or service and you feel that there is no way to satisfy this person long-term, it makes sense to say goodbye to that customer too. You can bet that this person is not spreading a good message about your store. You'll feel better once you sever the tie.

When faced with letting a customer go, do so politely and without malice. The conversation might go something like: "Bill, we've tried to work with you and we appreciate the business you've done with us in the past, but frankly we can't afford to sell to you any longer. You're a top-notch negotiator and it's left us in a position that we lose money when we sell to you. Like I said we appreciate the business we've done before, but we can no longer sell to you in the way that we've done in the past."

Or another example, "Jane, we've not been able to make you happy. We feel that we've made out best effort and are asking you to take your business elsewhere. Perhaps they can satisfy you. Thanks for your patronage in the past."

A slow paying customer is yet another reason for reexamination of your relationship with him. When it comes to customers and certain business, there really is a time when it's better to say goodbye.

Ain't no mountain high enough.

Excerpt from Wikipedia:

*"**Ain't No Mountain High Enough**" is an <u>R&B</u>/<u>soul</u> <u>song</u> written by <u>Nickolas Ashford & Valerie Simpson</u> in 1966 for the <u>Tamla Motown</u> label. The composition was first successful as a 1967 hit <u>single</u> recorded by <u>Marvin Gaye</u> and <u>Tammi Terrell</u>, becoming a hit again in 1970 when recorded by former <u>Supremes</u> frontwoman <u>Diana Ross</u>. The song became Ross' first solo number-one hit on the <u>Billboard Hot 100</u> chart and was nominated for a <u>Grammy Award</u>.*

If you happened to have picked up this book as part of a process in determining whether you will proceed with starting a business of your own, thank you! I guess owning a business is kind of an American Dream, isn't it? It doesn't appeal to everybody, of course, for some are just more comfortable with the security that an 8 to 5 offers. That's all good, but if part of your vision for your future is to own a business, then first know this...it isn't easy! In fact, the odds against the success for any new business are staggering...they are mountain high. Consider this: 4 out of 5 new businesses don't last 5 years and of the ones that do, 8 out of ten of those fail in the next 5 years.

That's a pretty high mountain isn't it? And yet I can tell you there are few things as rewarding as bringing something to fruition and then continuing to mold and massage the initial concept until it becomes profitable.

If you were wondering why so many businesses fail, I would guess much of it is due to naivety. Over estimating potential and demand, underestimating competition and expenses and being under financed at inception would all rank high on the list of probable causes of business failure. Couple that with the stresses that accompanies working through the things I just described and it's easy to see how some businesses are financially forced out while other entrepreneurs eventually just raise a white flag of surrender in reaction to circumstances.

So am I advising you against starting a business of your own? Quite the contrary, I can tell you there's nothing better than profiting fully from your own efforts and ideas. Maximizing your opportunity for success however requires a lot of groundwork on your part. Study all competitors in the arena in which you intend to operate. Understand what will make your offering unique and make your store a likely choice above the others. Utilize a consultant familiar with your type of operation and request demographic data to determine if there is sufficient demand in the surrounding area. Determine what you will need to survive for 3 years without income from your business. It is likely that it will take at least that long to launch your venture.

Starting a business is something analogous to climbing a mountain. From the bottom a mountain appears beautiful and appealing. And if you've ever experienced the view from the top you know that there's nothing like it. But if we had to climb the mountain to afford that mountaintop view it is unlikely many of us would ever see it. The challenge of a mountain climb and the view after its successful completion, however, is probably something that is quite rewarding, I can only speculate.

The thought of owning one's own business is quite appealing too. The climb from inception to success is also arduous. The feeling of success and the view from that perspective is also unequaled.

Family tradition.

Excerpt from Wikipedia:

*"**Family Tradition**" is a song written and recorded by American [country music](#) artist [Hank Williams, Jr..](#) It was released in May 1979 as the fourth and final single from his 1978 album of the [same name](#). It peaked at #4, and is one of his most popular songs.*

I was visiting with a customer-in-the-making for our company last week. He was second generation in the family business, his father having started the business in the 60s. It was with a great deal of pride that he guided us down the hallway pointing at pictures of his father's first stab at the business those many years ago. The son was rightfully proud of what he had accomplished too, taking his father's dream and building it into a formidable entity.

His is not a unique story. Many of the businesses we deal with are family legacies. Others are legacies from pioneers of hard work who coincidentally weren't family. I think the message here is really cool. Remember that the hard work you're doing today, next week, next month isn't just for you and those currently served by your endeavors. Rather, your efforts may affect people for several generations.

Business founding entrepreneurs are something special. They are likely visionary and often courageous. They sometimes start with little more than a dream but somehow the gifted and shrewd survive and live to sell another day.

Mitchell and Petz

We are working with another company that is over 100 years old. This company is in the process of writing an anniversary book that honors the hard work and diligence of those who have gone before. I am proud to say that we are involved in a small way in that project. When I look at the predecessors' pictures in that book or in the hall that I described earlier I realize that those pioneers dreamed dreams just as you and I do. They were concerned with sales and margin and payroll just as you and I are. I am quite sure there were times, when they questioned themselves and what they were doing, but they persevered.

One day in the distant future, if we're lucky, I mean really, really lucky, if we stay the course and if we too are diligent then perhaps our pictures will be in someone's book or on someone's wall. Here's to hoping it's not the post offices'.

I started a joke.

Excerpt from Wikipedia

*"**I Started a Joke**" is a 1968 song by the <u>Bee Gees</u> from their album <u>Idea</u>, which was released in September of that year. Curiously, it was not released as a single in the <u>UK</u>, where buyers who could not afford the album had to content themselves with a <u>Polydor</u> version by Heath Hampstead.*

I like jokes and joking around, don't you? I think a lot of people do. One thing I've noticed though is sometimes jokes just aren't appropriate in retail stores. I have been shocked by the insensitive remarks that I have heard in some of the stores I've shopped and worked...perhaps you have too. We can't control what is said everywhere, but as a storeowner or manager you certainly have the power to control what type of atmosphere is maintained in your place of business.

Don't get me wrong. I'm not talking about light-hearted banter. Joking around with customers can be fun and actually I believe most places would be improved by creating such an atmosphere. Fun is fun; I'm all for it, and I can guarantee that fun makes a work day go faster.

No! I'm referring specifically to the attempts at humor that are leveled at particular groups of people, whether those groups represent sexes, ethnic groups, or religions. If we want to get right down to it, there probably isn't a good place for crude and insensitive humor, but I know for a fact that it can be deadly in a retail environment. Offend one person and that person will tell others of the affected group.

If you want your store to succeed, it needs to appeal to as many people as you can bring in the door. I can assure you that your business will be ill served by alienating or offending any group. Retail can be long and hard. It's OK and important to culture an atmosphere of fun. So laugh, be friendly, find humor in the mundane and encourage your employees to do the same. But when it comes to jokes, make it absolutely clear what you will and what you will not tolerate.

Take it to the limit.
Excerpt from Wikipedia

*"**Take It to the Limit**" is a song by the <u>Eagles</u> from their fourth album, <u>One of These Nights</u>, written by <u>Randy Meisner</u>, <u>Don Henley</u> and <u>Glenn Frey</u>. The third single from the album, it was released on November 15, 1975, and went to #4 on the U.S. <u>Billboard Hot 100</u>. It was also the Eagles' greatest success to that point in the UK, with the single going to #12 on the charts.*

"Take It to the Limit" was sung by bassist <u>Randy Meisner</u>. It is a slow ballad about lost love and loneliness. It was the first and only A-side of a single on which he sang lead. It was also the first time neither Don Henley nor Glenn Frey sang lead on the A-side of a single. The single version is 3:48 in length, close to one minute shorter than the album version. It is the last single to feature founding member <u>Bernie Leadon</u> before he was replaced by guitarist <u>Joe Walsh</u>.

The primary concern of any retailer is profitability. If it's not, it should be. There are good altruistic rationales for being in the business...things like providing for the community and furnishing comfortable lifestyles for those who work for you. Selfless motivators are great, but let's face it, If your store isn't profitable, you can't begin to fulfill your altruistic goals let alone take care of yourself and your family.

Therefore it is imperative that your store produces a profit! Now on the cusp that might seem to fall in the "well-duh" category, but don't dismiss the thought prematurely. For a number of years there has been a focus on being price competitive and for good reason. Shoppers are very savvy and better informed than at any other point in the past. But there have been a number of businesses that were singularly focused on price that have failed. Those failures perhaps confirming a number of studies that have indicated that price falls farther down the list of "reasons why we buy" than one would initially expect.

Here's the point. It might not be a bad idea to examine taking your margins to the limit. I'll wager you're not there yet. Pricing and the concept of price image is a lot of smoke and mirrors. You have to create the image of competitive prices. Use gondola flags to point to your best prices on every counter. Use your end caps to display good prices on low-ticket items. Brag about your pricing, remembering that you're conjuring an image...an image that is anchored to the perception of value. If you are offering services, selection and convenience as value-added qualities, make sure that your prices reflect the resources that it takes to deliver those values. In other words, don't be afraid to raise prices.

One final thought: There will be only one lowest-price provider in any retail arena...make sure that you're not him.

Turn! Turn! Turn!

Excerpt from Wikipedia

"Turn! Turn! Turn! (to Everything There Is a Season)", *often abbreviated to* **"Turn! Turn! Turn!"**, *is a* <u>song</u> *adapted entirely from the* <u>Book of Ecclesiastes</u> *in the Bible (with the exception of the last line) and put to music by* <u>Pete Seeger</u> *in 1959. Seeger waited until 1962 to record his own version of it, releasing the song on his* <u>The Bitter and the Sweet</u> *album on* <u>Columbia Records</u>.[1]

The song became an international <u>hit</u> *in late 1965 when it was* <u>covered</u> *by the American* <u>folk rock</u> *band* <u>The Byrds</u>, *reaching #1 on the* <u>Billboard Hot 100</u> *chart and #26 on the* <u>UK Singles Chart</u>. *Many biblical scholars believe that Ecclesiastes 1:1 implies* <u>King Solomon</u> *(born c. 1011 BC) as the book's author, but regardless of its precise origins, The Byrds' version of the song easily holds the record for the number 1 hit with the oldest lyrics.*

One of the traditional ways of looking at profitability is to examine inventory turns. Inventory turns are analyzed as a yearly indicator and can give insight as to how effectively your Inventory investment is working for you.

Simply stated, inventory turns represent the number of time you "sell through" and replace your inventory during the year.

- Inventory turns = Cost of Goods Sold ÷ Average Inventory @ Cost

Obviously the idea is to increase the number of turns so that you can produce an equal amount of profit off of a smaller inventory investment. The money that would have been invested in inventory resulting in a lower turn rate could be invested into other categories of inventory or other investments.

Here's the problem: Many people become singularly focused on inventory turns and reach for extreme figures. Extreme inventory turn figures probably signal out of stocks and missed sales based upon customers not finding what they want when they want it. For example a shopper comes into your store needing 5 widgets...you fill in the item name...she finds only 3. More than likely she does not buy the 3 you have but will instead go somewhere with a deeper stock of whatever she's looking for. In this case of sales lost, you may not even be aware that there was a problem. You review your inventory figures feeling all warm and fuzzy about the turns you have produced, pop your arm out of place patting yourself on the back and unfortunately, completely miss the cash deposit that you could have made.

It's important to review turns and to try to achieve moderate turn levels. Just make sure that you don't TURN yourself into out of stock situations, TURN your customers away and TURN your back on additional profit opportunities.

What's a good goal for turns? Kind of depends on your industry. For example average inventory turns in the retail hardware business is around 2.5 or 2.6. Check industry reports within your category offering or keep track of turns on a yearly basis and try to raise your own performance bar.

You've lost that lovin' feeling.

Excerpt from Wikipedia

"You've Lost That Lovin' Feelin'" *is a 1964 song by* <u>The Righteous Brothers</u> *which became a number-one hit single in the* <u>United States</u> *and the* <u>United Kingdom</u> *the following year. In 1999, the performing-rights organization Broadcast Music, Inc. (BMI) ranked the song as having had more radio and television play in the United States than any other song during the 20th century.[2] Additionally, the song was chosen as one of the* <u>Songs of the Century</u> *by* <u>RIAA</u> *and ranked #34 on the list of the* <u>500 Greatest Songs of All Time</u> *by* <u>Rolling Stone</u>.

We were working with a client the other day and reviewing the dramatic decline in his business's volume over the past five years. It is no secret that the economy has fostered some of the decline that has occurred with his and others within his industry. But what was more interesting was the fact that his store's decline started long before the 2009 bust.

We discussed the "pre-bust" decline and the storeowner and his manager recounted customers that they had lost during that period. They described various reasons for the "disconnects" with customers they had experienced. As Gary and I listened we glanced at each other, eyebrows raised. Our eyebrows were raised because we had had a pre-consult meeting in which we discussed what we thought was poor customer service and poor attitudes from the top down in this store. It seemed that arrogance and egos were prevalent and even perhaps, for reasons neither of us understood, held in esteem.

It is important for every store manager to realize that his customers have choices. There are times when you may feel compelled to be impolite and less than service oriented. Let's face it. There are people that make being polite hard every time they walk in to your store. But in this store, the less than friendly attitudes were a rule and not an exception and they had already taken a toll. We stressed that customers are a privilege and not an inconvenience.

In the conversations that followed with this dealer we suggested that a customer list of "then and now" be contrasted and efforts made to contact those who had been lost. We even suggested that perhaps apologies or whatever it took to mend fences were in order. The manager bit his lip, but nodded his head in acknowledgment of this sad retrospective look at his operation.

Here's the thing. Not all people are people-people. But if you are going to organize a staff that will excel in retail, it sure is beneficial to keep this thought in mind. I once had a retailer tell me he hated dealing with his customers and would be much happier if he was working alone on a tractor or in the field. It was apparent from his operation that his customers would have liked it better too.

Remember as manager you set the tone for customer service and the attitude toward it. Evaluate yours today.

(They long to be) close to you.

Excerpt from Wikipedia

*"**(They Long to Be) Close to You**" is a popular song written by <u>Burt Bacharach</u> and <u>Hal David</u>. It was first recorded by <u>Richard Chamberlain</u> and released as a single in <u>1963</u> as "They Long to Be Close to You", without parentheses. However, it was the single's flip side, "<u>Blue Guitar</u>", that became a hit. The tune was also recorded as a demo by <u>Dionne Warwick</u> in 1963 and re-recorded with a <u>Burt Bacharach</u> arrangement for her 1964 album <u>Make Way for Dionne Warwick</u>, and was released as the <u>B-side</u> of her 1965 single "Here I Am". Bacharach released his own version in 1968. But the version recorded by <u>The Carpenters</u>, which became a hit in 1970, is the best known.*

This Carpenter's song title holds a great message for owners and managers of smaller retail businesses. As a business expands and prospers there are more reasons for an owner or manager to separate himself from the activity. There are so many balls that must be juggled that it seems to just make sense to isolate an office and have solitude and serenity within which to study and make decisions. An office located in this fashion just naturally separates the manager from what's going on and particularly from her patrons.

Perhaps you'd better reconsider, particularly if you're operating a store thats success is driven by personal relationships and interactions. And when you think about it like that you should probably begin to see that most small to moderate size retail stores fall into this category. Does that mean that you, as owner or manager, should regularly work the sales floor? There truly may not be time for that, but that's too bad. Just like the song lyrics say, customers long to be close to you or at least acknowledged by you and therein lays the secret. If you make it clear to me that I as a customer am appreciated and important to your store's success, I am likely to continue to deal with you. All of us like to be known and appreciated!

Of course, if you are not naturally a people person and flat out just don't feel comfortable with the interactions that I have described above, perhaps you need to have a manager figure who takes that responsibility off of your shoulders. Still, the higher in the chain of command an acknowledgement comes from the better.

During a consult, I once had a manager of a small lumberyard tell me that she was the only one her customers would deal with. Of course, this is an even worse situation and probably reflected her lack of skill at personnel development. Don't confuse this type of saddling that can occur with a manager or owner who regularly acknowledges and expresses appreciation to her patrons as they pass through. Remember, they long to be close to you!

Rockin' Retail Lessons

I've just gotta get a message to you.

Excerpt from Wikipedia

*"**I've Gotta Get a Message to You**" is a song recorded by the Bee Gees in 1968, which became their second number-one single on the UK Singles Chart, and reached number eight on the US pop chart. In the United Kingdom the song was released as a single only.*

The song appeared on the US edition of the Bee Gees' third album Idea, however not in the United Kingdom the Vince Melouney track "Such a Shame" appeared instead. in the UK but both songs are featured on the CD edition released circa 1991.

This song was sent to Atlantic Records with "I Laugh in Your Face", therefore it would be reasonable to assume that the latter was the intended B-side. However, it was dropped in favour of Kitty Can.

I recently had the honor of speaking at the National Hardware Show in Las Vegas. My presentation was titled "More Effective Marketing" and I wish you could have been there!

Marketing is a difficult process for any retailer and understanding what she's trying to market is critical. One facet of marketing is advertising, and yes I believe there are differences between marketing and advertising. Advertising, I believe, is product specific while marketing is all about communicating your brand. Brand? Well, my belief is that brand is all things, both good and bad, by which your company is identified. The ideal marketing, then, focuses on building up the good and shifting focus from those things that aren't.

But let's concentrate the next few moments on advertising. Advertising, according to the American Marketing Association is a "form of communication that persuades people to purchase a product or a service". I often joke that some retailers have told me that, if such is the case, then they have never advertised because their ads have failed to persuade anybody to buy anything. When talking with our customers we hear their frustration regarding advertising and it's easy to see that effective advertising is truly a science.

Let's fast forward past the content of the advertisement (perhaps I'll write about it in another article). For now, let's say that we've got our killer-diller ad, how do we get that message to the people we're trying to reach? I taught during a seminar at Las Vegas the elements of time and space as regards advertising.

For example, I place my advertisement in the Friday issue of a local paper; this is the issue that my representative has advised me has the highest circulation. Some people read the issue Friday night, perhaps, but others won't get to it until Saturday or even Sunday. My offer has to be strong enough to pull those people through time. In other words, if prospects read the issue Saturday and do not react at that time, my offer has to pull them to at least Monday of the following week. And when you think about it, regardless of when they read it, the offer has to pull them through some element of time, doesn't it?

Now let's talk about space. If that same advertisement is read by someone 8 miles from my store, the offer must now be strong enough to pull the reader through space...8 miles to be exact.

Rockin' Retail Lessons

Couple the issue of time and space together and you can see the natural erosion that occurs in my message.

The primary thing to remember about these two elements is the strength of the offer. The second consideration is that the communication should probably occur several times, rather than just as a one-time shot. Also try and support all of your advertising efforts with banners and in-store signage to complete the communication circle. Make sure all of your employees are fully aware and prepared to sell the sale items and also the critical associated items that can help you increase the diminished margin necessitated by making a strong offer.

Advertising is important to a successful retail store and so as regards my operation, "I've just got to get a message to you"!

Ricki don't lose that number.

Excerpt from Wikipedia

"Rikki Don't Lose That Number" *is a single released in* _1974_ *by rock/pop/jazz group* _Steely Dan_ *and the opening track of their third album* _Pretzel Logic_. *It was the most successful single of the group's career, peaking at #4 on the* _Billboard Hot 100_ *in the summer of 1974.*[1]

When you gather customer information you are, no doubt, gathering names, address and phone numbers. But are you missing mining the gold that exists in email addresses? The ways in which we communicate are changing rapidly. If you're not using email campaigns as part of your advertising efforts you are missing golden opportunities.

When we design a website for a customer, email capabilities are built-in functions. We author the site to allow subscribers to opt-in and opt-out and the database is automatically maintained by the application. This also keeps our customers compliant with anti-spamming regulations.

OK obviously the first step involved in launching an email campaign is compiling an email list. As I suggested if yours is a business in which you ask for information in order to set up accounts include an email address as a required field. If yours is a cash business and you don't use customer numbers, then get creative. Offer a coupon with email newsletter sign up. Email can be configured with auto-responders so that once you have entered the email address into your database an email coupon is automatically generated and sent.

Don't overdo it. Limit your email "newsletters" and offers to once a month or so and never share the email address for any purpose. I always suggest offering informational pieces along with your offers and make sure that there is a link by which a receiver can opt-out at will.

There are large well-known companies who are using email as their primary means of advertising and communication. It's easy to see why. Once an email management system is in place the costs for campaigns are minimal. Further, an email campaign can be conceived, written and distributed in hours.

To make an email campaign even more effective, include links that direct back to your website. This will improve your website traffic and allow you yet another way to communicate. Perhaps a special offer coupon can be printed from the website. The idea is to tell your story, make an offer and then encourage further communication. All of these points are well served by email marketing.

Our email systems allow the user to watch the effectiveness of the campaign, showing for example how many of the emails were actually opened. Many, of course, will be immediately deleted. This is no different from any other type of advertisement. The primary difference is that you will know how many emails are actually opened and therefore be able to study your subject lines to see what works more effectively. With this type of feedback, you would be able to continue to tweak for optimum results.

So if this song is ever rerecorded I suggest its title be changed to "Ricci Don't Lose That Email"

Black water.

Excerpt from Wikipedia

"Black Water" *is a song by the* <u>American</u> *music group* <u>The Doobie Brothers</u> *from the album* <u>What Were Once Vices Are Now Habits</u>. *Released in* <u>1974</u>, *it features* <u>Patrick Simmons</u> *on lead vocals.*

Introducing a <u>bluegrass</u> *sound to traditional* <u>rock</u>, *"Black Water" hit #1 on the* <u>Billboard Hot 100</u> *on 15 March 1975. The song was originally released in early 1974 as the* <u>B-side</u> *to "Another Park, Another Sunday" but according to Tom Johnston in the Live at Wolftrap DVD, radio stations withdrew "Another Park, Another Sunday" from airplay because of the words ".. radio brings me down .. ", and "Black Water" ultimately became the more popular song.*[1]

Want to know a sure way to alienate your female customers? There's probably a laundry list of ways to do that, but I know for sure that ill-kempt restrooms are a deal killer for most of your female customers and, truth be known, probably a lot of your macho male ones as well. Let's face it, when nature calls, there's just something pretty disgusting about restrooms that are not properly maintained.

Mitchell and Petz

Perhaps you're exasperated and wondering what in the world is an article about maintaining restrooms doing in a retail lesson book. I can tell you most certainly that as a manager trainee for the TG&Y stores company, a successful discount chain of the 70s, it was one of the first lessons learned. Managers were trained to see to it that the cleaning process was scheduled and adhered to religiously. This is the simplest of lessons, perhaps the most basic one in this book and further, possibly, one that could have or should have been omitted. But when you think about it, what you are trying to do is capture a competitive edge. Sometimes a competitive edge is honed by the simplest of actions.

I once had a manager tell me that he didn't encourage his customers to use his store's facilities anyway. Come on. Give me a break! The whole idea is to create an atmosphere in which people feel welcomed and are comfortable and will feel encouraged to return. Have shoddily maintained restrooms, or worse yet, ones that you don't make readily available to them and see how fast your customer count declines.

Of course, the essence of the message here should not be limited to restrooms, but rather should permeate to your entire operation. I believe, however, that sometimes clutter and even a spot of dust here or there is much more likely to be tolerated anywhere other than the privy. Make sure that you have regularly scheduled bathroom maintenance and a system for monitoring them between scheduled cleanings.

I can see clearly now.

Excerpt from Wikipedia

*"**I Can See Clearly Now**" is a Billboard Hot 100 Chart #1 hit <u>song</u>, written and recorded by <u>Johnny Nash</u>. It was a single from the album of the same name and achieved success in the <u>United States</u> and the <u>United Kingdom</u> when it was released in 1972. It was covered by many artists throughout the years, including a 1993 hit version by <u>Jimmy Cliff</u>, who re-recorded it for the motion picture soundtrack of <u>Cool Runnings</u>, where it reached the top 20 at #18 on the Billboard Hot 100.*

Take a look around your store. Does it look as big as it really is? Or if your store is small, the better question is, does it look as big as it **can**? The primary reason it is important to make your store look as big as possible is simple. People associate the size of a store with their perception of its selection. It makes sense doesn't it? A bigger store typically has more products and offers more choices than a smaller one so it's easy to understand why people would make that assumption.

There are several ways to make a store look bigger. Let's talk about a couple. When we are designing a store, we always look for ways to open up the longest vistas. In some cases this means creating diagonal aisles from the entrance doors to the back corners. These aisles will normally be the longest ones we can introduce. In addition we suggest aligning gondolas in a fashion that allows people to view the full length of the sales area from as many locations as possible. Sometimes, because of room dimensions, these tactics will not work, but more often they do!

There are other ways to make your showroom look bigger. One way is to use lower gondolas. This is a controversial point because it is also important to maximize inventory dollars per square foot to increase opportunities. I understand that and I clearly see both sides of the argument, but remember that right now we're talking about making your store look bigger. So, at least consider the possibility of lowering your displays. Who knows, perhaps it might even produce the added benefit of motivating you to clean up slow moving merchandise and more closely mange your inventory turns and sales floor productivity. Another certain benefit is helping to control theft.

Anyway, for right now, let's say that you determine that your store might benefit from lowering the gondolas to 60 or 66 inches. Once you have lowered them, make sure that your products do not extend above! Move your taller products to the walls. This will give your store nice neat lines plus open up vistas of the perimeter. Consider adding wall décor images to draw customers' eyes to those walls and I guarantee you that your store will appear to be larger.

I got a name.

Excerpt from Wikipedia

*"**I Got a Name**" is a 1973 single recorded by <u>Jim Croce</u> and written by Norman Gimbel and Charles Fox. It was released in 1973 and was the first single from <u>his album of the same title</u>. It reached a peak of 10 on the Billboard Hot 100 after spending 17 weeks on the chart. "I Got a Name" was also the theme song for the 1973 movie <u>The Last American Hero</u>. It was also featured in the movies <u>The Ice Storm</u> and <u>Invincible</u>.*

What's in a name? I've heard it said that to almost everyone the sound of one's own name is the sweetest sound there is. Don't really know about that, I think I'd rather listen to some good music than somebody chanting my name. Guess it might depend on the chanter, but that's another story. Anyway a person's name is nonetheless very important.

But what about a business...what's in a businesses' name? Well, a lot I think. This particular lesson is not about the name you chose for your business, we're probably too late for that subject. But you know what drives us crazy when we go in to help a business over a hump or to make a good one even better? It's not the name of the business, but the fact that the name is conspicuously absent in the retail space.

If you're in your store right now, look around. How many times do you see your businesses' name? Think it's not important? How often does someone say, who do I make this check out to?

Mitchell and Petz

Where am I? Earth to storeowner, earth to storeowner: you spend hundreds, even thousands of dollars a month to bring people into your store. Perhaps you advertise on television or the radio. Or perhaps your advertising is more print- based...doesn't matter; you are spending big bucks to bring people into your store. Does it make any sense at all to abandon your message once the people get there? It's ludicrous isn't it?

You have a wonderful opportunity to communicate with people while they are on your turf. You need to tell them about your services, your products, and your value. Let them know what makes your store unique. Go ahead, brag about it. This is one time mom would approve. But for the love of heaven, your store has a name...make sure you use it.

Shout.

Excerpt from Wikipedia

*"**Shout**" is a 1984 song by the <u>British</u> band <u>Tears for Fears</u>. Written by <u>Roland Orzabal</u> and <u>Ian Stanley</u> and sung by Orzabal (with <u>Curt Smith</u> duetting on the chorus), it was the band's eighth single release (the second taken from their second LP <u>Songs from the Big Chair</u>) and sixth <u>UK Top 40</u> hit, peaking at #4 in January <u>1985</u>. In the USA, it reached #1 on the <u>Billboard Hot 100</u> on 3 August 1985 and remained there for three weeks. "Shout" would become one of the most successful <u>pop</u> songs of 1985, eventually reaching the Top Ten in 25 countries.*

If you were to shout at me, what would be the purpose of the shouting? I can only think of a few reasons why anybody would shout at someone else. You might shout at me if you wanted to get my attention. You might shout if there was a lot of other noise in the environment and you had to talk at that level to be heard. And finally you might shout at me if you just wanted to make a strong point.

When you think about it you may come to the conclusion that advertising and shouting have a lot in common. For example, if you want to get customers and would-be customers attention, you advertise. You shout. If you want your message to be heard above the noise that your competitors are making, you advertise. You shout. If you want to make a strong point about an attribute of your selection, your price, your services or your personnel you advertise. You shout.

How can going through the mental exercise of associating advertising with shouting help you? Think about this: When you shout you put passion and energy into the act. It requires effort. Do you approach advertising the same way or do you go through the motions and simply complete the process for sake of completion. Perhaps you use a "well it's better than nothing philosophy". I would challenge that thought and say if your message only whispers perhaps it isn't better than nothing and maybe it is exactly nothing...albeit nothing that costs you money.

To advertise successfully filter each proposed advertising interaction through this question: "Does it shout"? If the answer is no, go back to the drawing board. Interrupting is the key attribute of a successful advertisement. An advertisement has to get peoples' attention. If you successfully interrupt your target customer you have a good chance at conveying your message, whatever the message is. The other attributes of a successful advertising campaign, engaging, informing, educating and making an offer, are secondary to the big enchilada...the super-sized burrito...the ultimate taco of interrupting.

Want to get my attention? Shout!

The letter.

Excerpt from Wikipedia.

*"**The Letter**" is a song written by* <u>*Wayne Carson Thompson*</u> *which was a #1 hit in 1967 for* <u>*The Box Tops.*</u>

It's almost a thing of the past, isn't it? The letter, I mean. Oh, don't get me wrong, you still get things through the mail (snail-mail, as I often see if referred to). Some things you want but most you don't. The delivery of messages, even personal correspondence has gone digital. How you feel about that change is probably directly related to your age.

From a retailer's perspective this change can be a good thing. A good thing, that is, if you choose to embrace the change and capitalize on it. Email newsletters can be a great cost effective way to stay in touch with your customer base. The rules of a successful email campaign are very similar to the rules of any good advertising...interrupt, educate, inform and make an offer. Do so with regularity and you will no doubt see results. In fact I know of one high profile interior décor chain that relies on this method as their total communication vehicle. I don't have permission to use their name so I won't, but I guarantee that you would recognize it.

There are certain restrictions and requirements for this type of campaign. You or someone on your behalf will have to understand the process. You won't want to send group emails that look like group emails. You will want the final product to look as personalized and polished as you can make it. This may involve special software or a third party to manage the process.

Because of the amount of Spam that in-boxes are bombarded with you will want to respect the wishes of your customers. But beyond their wishes are also laws that govern this type of email process. Basic considerations include making it clear that the customer understands that she is signing up for an email campaign. It is also important to provide an easy opt-out process. Doing so with each mailing will ensure that if a recipient changes her mind she can opt-out with ease.

A good email advertising campaign requires effort. It requires a give and take process. If your customer is going to take the time to read it then she will require that you offer something of substance. Substantive offers should include information and education, but they will also require that you make legitimate offers in the form of give-a-ways or price concessions. You may require your customers to print out a coupon that is included on the mailing. Even though the delivery method is evolving, the old tried and true coupon approach still works. A couple of parting thoughts: make the offer time specific. A time specific offer will produce more response than one that is open ended.

Don't expect the first mailing to produce huge results. Like other forms, email advertising requires frequency and repetition. Your results will probably depend on the age demographic of your clientele but you just may find an exciting new venue for your communication process.

Twist and shout.

Excerpt from Wikipedia:

*"**Twist and Shout**" is a song written by <u>Phil Medley</u> and <u>Bert Russell</u>. It was originally titled "Shake It Up, Baby" and recorded by the Top Notes and then covered by <u>The Isley Brothers</u>. It was covered by <u>The Beatles</u> with <u>John Lennon</u> on the lead vocals and originally released on their first album <u>Please Please Me</u>. The song was covered by <u>The Mamas & the Papas</u> in the style of a ballad in 1967 on their album <u>Deliver</u>, and on a film soundtrack by <u>Cliff Richard</u>.*

What have you changed about your store recently? Do you constantly innovate? First things first: don't let the word innovation scare you. Innovation is no more than change. Some innovations turn out to be good things, some innovations fail. It doesn't matter. The important thing is that you foster change.

Change is always good but not all changes are. Think about that one for a moment and see if your head starts spinning like Linda Blair's. Change is good because it keeps you looking for improvement. It keeps your operation dynamic. Of course, you'll create some changes that ultimately won't work. Evaluate each failure to determine if the fundamental principle was wrong or just the execution. Perhaps with some tweaking the failed change can be salvaged. If not, look on it as a learning experience and start examining other possibilities for modification.

Mitchell and Petz

I have read about an interesting concept. Don't remember where, but the basic idea was this: if you're looking for innovation look to someone who knows nothing about what you're doing. The premise is that an outsider does not bring the predetermined structure that sometimes paralyzes those in the know. It's interesting, if nothing more. It actually kind of makes sense to me I must admit.

If you're wondering what all of this has to do with this lesson's title, here you go. I thought that change was well represented by the word twist. If you change something, you twist it up. Now for the shout part: If you make dramatic changes to your store or operations you must tell your customers...shout it to them. Shout it in the form of any advertising you do. If you make subtle changes shout them to your employees to make sure they understand the rationale and benefits.

So go ahead, shake it up baby...twist and shout!

Build me up buttercup.

Excerpt from Wikipedia

"Build Me Up Buttercup" *is the name of a song written by* Mike d'Abo *and* Tony Macaulay, *and released by* The Foundations *with* Colin Young *singing the lead vocals in 1968. This was the third major hit for The Foundations. Colin Young replaced* Clem Curtis *in 1968 and this was the first Foundations hit that he sang on. It reached number 2 on the UK charts and number 3 in the US on the Billboard Hot 100, where it stayed for 11 weeks.*

A friend of mine, whom we consult with on a regular basis, recently sent me notes he had taken during his attendance at a presentation which gave instruction for dealing with the personality traits of different age groups. The groups were broken down like this: The Matures, born between 1909 and 1945, the Baby Boomers, born between 1946 and 1964 (I'm in this group), the Generation Xers, born between 1965 and 1979, and finally the Millenials, those born between 1980 and 2000. The presenter characterized personality traits of each group and intimated how social and economic events shaped those traits.

Perhaps in the work force, the Millenials have been maligned and the presenter characterized them this way: They've known affluence their whole lives, they want immediate gratification, and they were very protected by their parents. He further characterized what the Millenials as a group wanted from their workplace: An individual who will help them achieve their goals;

Open, constant communication and positive reinforcement from their boss; A job that provides personal fulfillment; and ways to shed the stress in their lives.

This was very interesting stuff and now that I've read what the Millenials are looking for, I've decided that I want to throw in with them. I think I want what they want. But after thinking about it further, I wondered if those things aren't really what we all want? Would anybody not want the assistance of someone who could help them reach their goals? Is there anybody out there that doesn't like positive reinforcement...a little stroking? How about personal fulfillment and ways to shed stress? I can't imagine that any of us would turn those things down given the offer. My point is that when you look at ways to compensate, motivate and retain employees, this would be a pretty good list to plan from and maybe even regardless of age.

I realize that there are differences in age groups. I remember that Tom Brokaw characterized The Matures as the "greatest generation" and each of us would have an opinion on that. It would be hard to argue with the sacrifices of the WWII or depression generations, but people are people. They seem to rise to their challenges. And when it comes right down to it, maybe there are more similarities than differences. And further, in my musings, I wondered if there's ever been a generation who didn't see the possibility of the next one going to "hell in a hand basket".

So, the next time you contemplate ways to motivate and retain your employees consider formulating your plan from the Millenials' view point. Who knows? It might just have you looking at things differently.

If you could read my mind.

Excerpt from Wikipedia:

"If You Could Read My Mind" *is a* song *by Canadian singer/songwriter* Gordon Lightfoot*. It reached number one on Canadian music charts and was his first recording to appear on the American music charts, reaching number 5 on the* Billboard Hot 100 *singles chart in January 1971. Later in the year, it reached number 30 in the UK. Lightfoot has cited his* divorce *for inspiring the* lyrics,[1] *saying they came to him as he was sitting in a vacant* Toronto *house one summer.*[2]

Well it probably wouldn't be a good thing most of the time would it? I mean reading each other's minds, of course. However reading minds might come in very handy when dealing with staff that you're trying to direct.

As consultants we regularly hear managers lament about what they see as problems in their businesses. And almost always high on their list is the fact that their personnel just don't get it. I'll leave it to you to fill in what the "it" is, could be almost anything. OK, here's a big scoop for you. If your employees don't get your direction, perhaps it's because the message has not been clearly communicated.

We regularly work with a high-ranking officer of a small chain of stores. He is challenged to clearly communicate his desires to his second in command and then have those directions carried out to his satisfaction. The easy reaction might be to say that his lieutenant is at fault, and since the failure is his, it's time to replace him. But, sadly, the company has many years and dollars invested in this employee. Rather than writing him off, to me, it makes sense to have a meeting of the minds and clearly outline expectations.

During our coaching we have recommended that when these meetings occur the supervisor has his subordinate repeat to him what he has heard as the directive. The next step would be to agree on a timetable for the responsibilities to be completed and then finally to follow up at the agreed upon times to check out progress.

There are probably some of you reading this who would say micro managing should not be necessary that at this level of an organization. And in an ideal world, of course, you would be right. But remember it's not currently working satisfactorily. Would it be better to simply cut bait and start over? I don't believe so and if you are charged with fixing a similar problem then communication is the key. In fact, it is the only possible answer to improving the situation and who knows, with better communication the working relationship may progress to the point that there will no longer be need for reading minds.

Listen to what the man said.

Excerpt from Wikipedia

"Listen to What the Man Said" *is a hit single from* <u>Wings</u>' *1975 album* <u>Venus and Mars</u>. *The song featured new member* <u>Joe English</u> *on drums, with guest musicians* <u>Dave Mason</u> *on guitar and* <u>Tom Scott</u> *on* <u>soprano saxophone</u>.[1] *It was a number 1 single on the* <u>Billboard Hot 100</u> *chart in the US;[2] as well, it reached number 1 in Canada on the* <u>RPM</u> *National Top Singles Chart.[3] It also reached number 6 in the UK, and reached the top ten in Norway and New Zealand and the top twenty in the Netherlands.[4][5] The single was certified Gold by the* <u>Recording Industry Association of America</u> *for sales of over one million copies.[6]*

How long has it been since you've conducted or have had others conduct customer surveys? We sometimes undertake them as part of a comprehensive store study that our company offers. They're not, in my opinion, a lot of fun to do, but I think they can be extremely informative.

One survey we conducted indicated that many people felt the staff unfriendly. Another indicated that women didn't feel that the store was very female friendly. You never know what you'll get but, on a lot of levels, it makes sense to find out.

There are a couple of reasons for this: 1. You will get a lot of good information. 2. Your customers will appreciate the fact that you're concerned about what they think.

Mitchell and Petz

When our company conducts the surveys we attack three fronts. Entrance, exit and phone interviews, and each has a specific purpose. During the entrance interviews we ask questions dealing with geography and awareness e.g. How far do you live from our store? How are you most familiar with us? During exit interviews we ask if they were looking for something specific. Did they find it? And if the answer is yes, did they buy it? And if that answer is no, then we ask them why not? E.g. was it a pricing issue? Was it a quality issue? Etc.

The phone interviews serve yet another purpose. Because we deal with a lot of home centers we ask for a list of current and also past customers. We attempt to learn why the former customers are no longer current customers. People are often very surprised that someone really cares what they think and therein lies part of the power of the interview process. We often learn some really interesting stuff and sometimes that interesting stuff is not good. That's what we're hoping for, of course, because you can't fix something if you don't know it's broken.

After you have your information gathered, analyze it. Look for reoccurring themes and comments. Assess whether there are things to which you should react. There probably will be.

Customer surveys are not fun, but if you want to improve your operation, listen to what the man said.

That smell.

Excerpt from Wikipedia

"That Smell" *is a song by the southern rock band* Lynyrd Skynyrd. *Written by* Ronnie Van Zant *and guitarist* Allen Collins, *it was released in 1977 on the album* Street Survivors. *At the time the song was written, the band had been drinking and doing many different drugs.[1] Van Zant had said that he started drinking heavily to relieve the pressure of performing in front of large audiences.[1]*

I'm not even familiar with this song myself, but it does bring up a great point that all retailers should be cognizant of. We have five senses that affect the way we interact with the world. The more of those senses that are favorably stimulated during a shopping trip the more positively the experience is regarded.

For example a store that is interesting visually commands our attention longer. If you command my attention longer you will keep me in your store longer. Keep me in your store longer and you're much more likely to persuade me to buy something. OK, check, sense number one, sight, covered.

Evaluate who constitutes your ideal customer and then play the music style that will appeal to that ideal. Get them rocking, whoever they are, and once again data confirms that their shop-times will increase. Remember everything is about appealing to the senses, because through the senses is the only way you can communicate with anybody.

Mitchell and Petz

That smell? Sure, aromas are a part of the experience too. That is one of the reasons we recommend serving coffee to customers in the morning and popcorn in the afternoon. There is just something about the smell of coffee in the morning that most people would assess positively.

We should mention the other two senses as well. Let's start with taste. I guess the popcorn kind of hits both of those senses right between the eyes...well if they had eyes, that is. And to those who boldly proclaim that taste would not affect anybody's assessment of a business. I would respectively answer that you are wrong. For example, before their demise when anybody asked me my favorite airline I quickly answered Mid-West and it was for one simple reason: the fresh baked chocolate chip cookies. I know, I know, it's not a great reason to make a buying decision but there's just something primal that bypasses all of my faculties of reason when someone mentions chocolate chip cookies to me.

Finally, the sense of touch can be excited by things to do in your store. Hold this, feel that, touch this; anyway, you get the point. And in fact, if I were trying to sell you something face to face, I would try to get you to hold the object yourself. It's a very effective sales technique.

Regarding the appealing to the senses, experiential is hot buzzword in retail today. A shopping trip is not a shopping trip but rather an experience. The only way to make a shopping trip experiential is through the senses. How's your store doing in that regard?

Color my world.

Excerpt from Wikipedia

*"**Colour My World**" is a song written by <u>American</u> musician <u>James Pankow</u>, one of the founding members of the <u>rock</u>/<u>jazz fusion</u> band <u>Chicago</u>. Part of Pankow's <u>Ballad for a Girl in Buchannon</u> <u>song cycle</u>/suite, it was recorded for their second album <u>Chicago</u>, also called Chicago II (1970). <u>Terry Kath</u> is heard in the lead vocal, and <u>Walter Parazaider</u> performs the highly recognizable flute solo.*

The song was initially released as the B-side to "<u>Make Me Smile</u>" in March 1970. It was re-released in June 1971 as the B-side to the re-release of "<u>Beginnings</u>"; this second single reached #7 on the U.S. <u>Billboard Hot 100</u>.

Did you know that there are companies whose sole purpose is studying the psychology of color and how it affects people? You probably do, it's really no big secret at all. Many color considerations are actually quite common knowledge. For example, I doubt that you have seen many restaurant interiors decorated in blue. Several studies have indicated that the color blue suppresses appetite. If you want to stimulate appetites, try red or orange. There are also other color associations that are deeply engrained into our subconscious. Red, for instance, is considered the color of passion...think Valentine's Day.

Another important point about color is that it can be extremely faddish. Don't think so? If you're old enough to remember

Coppertone appliances you'll immediately react with an "oh, yeah"! If you're not that old think harvest gold, avocado green or poppy red. Current safer colors like almond, black and stainless steel will probably see their popularity wane in their due time.

My point is that color is fun, but it needs to be changed occasionally. I have been in stores that apparently invested in updated environments ten years ago that look quite dated today. Take a look around. Guilty as charged? If so, consider a face-lift. Paint is not terribly expensive and you really can quite literally transform an environment in short order. There are a number of resources--books, magazines, and web sites for example that can give you ideas about the psychology of color. Even if you don't buy into the idea of colors affecting people one way or the other, change can do you good. It can reenergize your staff and give your customers something new to notice and talk about.

One last note directed specifically at those of you whose stores are awash in beige. Beige floors, beige walls, beige fixtures! Come on, good grief! Have some fun! Put some color in your life! Sure faddish colors will change. You'll have to redo the environment eventually, but what a great way to signal to your customers that your store is new and relevant.

I do it for love.

Excerpt from Wikipedia

Do It for Love *is the sixteenth studio album by* <u>pop</u> *duo* <u>Hall & Oates</u>, *released in 2003. The title track peaked at #1 on Adult Contemporary charts making it the 8th #1 hit of their career, and "Forever For You", "Man on a Mission", and "Getaway Car" all charted as well.*

I just had a wonderful dining experience. No, not at an exclusive upscale restaurant and if fact, nothing could be further from the truth. My wife and I had $4.99 pizza buffets at CiCi's Pizza. It was only the 2nd or 3rd time I had eaten at one of the chain locations and I don't know much about their operation, but I do know this chain does a lot of things right.

Tonight, from Rachel, who greeted us and also handled our transaction, to each person staffing the buffet line, clear down to the young man who regularly and politely bused our table, there was something different about them. They genuinely seemed to understand their roles and be enjoying their jobs. Wow...how refreshing!

I can tell you one thing for certain: the collective employee attitude that permeated both of the CiCi locations I have tried is no accident! It wasn't just a bunch of employees who had been miraculously hired when heavenly constellations were aligned just right. No, it was a system of training and reward. No doubt, the training communicated the expectation of creating just such an atmosphere but I'll wager there were some reward factors at play as well. Now wait a minute, I'm not necessarily talking about financial incentives, although there may have been some of those.

I'm talking about the atmosphere of teamwork that is being cultivated. When one feels part of a team...I mean really part of a team...that person strives to not let the other members of the team down. They perform, if you'll excuse my slight hyperbole, out of love and respect for those with, and for, whom they work. Darn it, it's just more fun to be part of a team than it is to go it alone anyway.

So here's a question for you. Are you working to establish an environment of people who love their jobs? Hold on, I think this is the big one Elizabeth. It starts with you. Do you genuinely love your job? It'll show one way or the other, you know? It will also reflect in the attitudes of your employees. Do you still have the zest that drove you to your position originally? If not it's time to recapture it. One way that I have found to rekindle my passion anytime I sense it waning is to learn something new...to simply get better at what I do. I'm almost willing to bet it will work for you to. Perhaps if you know that your attitude is not where it needs to be, you should read a book on fostering teamwork.

OK, I'll close with a cliché that is just drenched in truth: Do what you love and you'll never have to work again. Oh, and one other thing, like they told us when we left the restaurant tonight, CiCi you later!

King of the road.

Excerpt from Wikipedia

"King of the Road" *is a 1964 song written and originally recorded by country singer* Roger Miller. *The lyrics tell of a* hobo *who despite being poor (a "man of means by no means") revels in his freedom, describing himself humorously as the "king of the road". It was Miller's fifth single for Smash Records.*[1]

If your store provides delivery or has a service team it's important to start thinking of the vehicles that you own as rolling billboards. It's yet another way to make a connection with current and potential customers. Now before you get ahead of me and say "Yeah, we've got our name on the sides of our trucks" and turn the page, read on and think about the scope of what I'm telling you.

First of all, there are a lot more possibilities today regarding mobile advertising than there has ever been before. Simple names, logos and phone numbers can readily be replaced by state of the art graphics and messages. Specialty printing companies can print decals and graphics that will get the attention of almost any breathing human being and I guess somewhere in that group is your target customer. The wonderful thing about this type of advertising is that once the initial cost is incurred you pay no further charges and every time you make a delivery and every time you make a service call, heck, even when your vehicles are sitting in your parking lot, they're serving a greater purpose.

If you have more than one vehicle there's no need to have each adorned with the same message. Perhaps you will advertise a niche product on the sides of one unit while speaking about special services offered on another. Put on your thinking cap and adhere to the same precepts that you ascribe to for any good marketing message. Consider what makes your operation different and if it's 7 day per week delivery, shout it on the side. If you have a specially manufactured doodad that offers benefits than no other doodad comes close to, tell that story. With computer and printing technologies advancing with such rapidity you will probably find that the costs will be far less than you might imagine. Therefore you can even consider changing the messages periodically.

I guess that's where a lesson about advertising and vehicles could end, but this one doesn't. It is extremely important that you hold whoever is in charge of vehicle maintenance to highest standards regarding cleanliness. Nothing speaks louder than a delivery vehicle that is in shoddy repair and unkempt. Unfortunately, in those cases, the message that is being shouted is not one that you want heard.

If I offered a child her choice of baubles I would almost bet she would pick the most sparkly one...make your vehicles sparkle. The people you're trying to attract are just big kids making choices.

Sittin' on the dock of the bay.

Excerpt from Wikipedia

"(Sittin' On) The Dock of the Bay" *is a song co-written by* [soul](#) *singer* [Otis Redding](#) *and guitarist* [Steve Cropper](#). *It was first recorded by Otis Redding in 1967, just days before his death. It was released posthumously on* [Stax Records](#)' *Volt label in 1968,[2] becoming the first posthumous single to top the charts in the US.[3] It charted at number 3 on the* [UK Albums Chart](#).

I don't know how many times I've walked into a store where we were called to consult only to find a clerk leaning on a sales counter, looking dreamily out the window or sitting, staring mindlessly at an entertaining Website. The latter, disguised as something productive, I'm quite sure. It drives me crazy. But whose fault is it anyway?

I've had managers tell me things like "When I hired Bobby I knew his limitations, knew what I was getting"...Really, you knew he was like that and you hired him anyway? Or "Well, Bobby's really not a self-starter. He'll do what I tell him, but I've got to line him out." Well, then for the love of heaven, line him out! Do so each morning and send Bobby home tired for a change.

In the retail environment there are always things that need to be done. Make sure that your Bobby knows that. Let him know that when there are no other clear responsibilities it is his job to grab a cloth and dust. Tell him to make sure that all gondolas look full and neat and that every label is facing outward so they are easily read. Tell him to make sure "talker" signs are hanging on side counters proudly conveying pricing, product features or warranty information. Teach him about impulse merchandising and have him maintain clip strips and end counters.

Very few independent retailers do adequate jobs of training. I guess that statement points a finger directly at the managers of those operations, but so be it. It is critical that payroll be kept in balance. In order to keep payroll in balance it is imperative that each employee understands her responsibilities and contributes accordingly.

Rockin' Retail Lessons

Tie a yellow ribbon.

Excerpt from Wikipedia

"Tie a Yellow Ribbon Round the Ole Oak Tree" *is a song by* <u>Dawn featuring Tony Orlando</u>, *written by* <u>Irwin Levine</u> *and* <u>L. Russell Brown</u> *and produced by* <u>Hank Medress</u> *and* <u>Dave Appell</u>. *It was a worldwide hit for the group in 1973.*

It reached number one on both the US and UK charts for four weeks in April 1973, number one on the Australian charts for seven weeks from May to July 1973 and number one on the New Zealand charts for ten weeks from June to August 1973. It was the top-selling single in 1973 in both the US and UK. In 2008, <u>Billboard</u> *ranked the song as the 37th biggest song of all time in its issue celebrating the 50th anniversary of the* <u>Hot 100</u>.[1]

I received my early managerial training with a company named TG&Y. For those of you not familiar with the company, it was a Chicago based early day variety store chain. The letters of the name were chosen based on the names of its founders... I believe they were Thompson, Gossen and Young. Anyway the company had a number of stores and during the seventies spanned across the country.

I was blessed during this basic training to work under one of the top-producing managers in the company. Richard ruled with an iron fist and it was definitely his way or the highway. In fact, his authoritarian style would probably not work in today's culture, but that's another story.

Near the start of the Christmas season, and yes by the way we did wait until after Thanksgiving back then. He would instruct us to have the clerks put big red ribbons on merchandise all over the store. He wasn't too particular about what items we put them on and told us not to be either. His point was that he wanted people to envision that nearly everything they saw in our store could be a great gift for someone. "Put the ribbons on everything and let them decide!" he would say. One side benefit we enjoyed was that when we placed enough big red bows around, the place really did look quite festive.

The point is that there are many holidays and special events. You can either choose to participate, and try to capture some of the extra sales these special days present, or not. If you choose to participate, you might try the big bow trick. Choose colors appropriate for the specific holiday. Red for Christmas, of course, but try pastels for mother's day, perhaps blue for father's day, or greens for St. Patrick's Day. You needn't make new bows every year. Save them in sealed containers and be ready to go for the next season. You might just drum up some business that you never even knew was possible.

Unforgettable.

Excerpt from Wikipedia

Unforgettable *is a* <u>popular</u> <u>song</u> *written by* <u>Irving Gordon</u>. *The song's original working title was Uncomparable. The music publishing company asked Irving to change it to Unforgettable. The song was published in* <u>1951</u>.

The most popular version of the song was recorded by <u>Nat King Cole</u> *in 1951, with an arrangement written by* <u>Nelson Riddle</u>.

The word is differentiation. Simply put it refers to the process by which you make your store different and therefore make it stand out. I have written a series of newsletters with a similar message and Gary and I teach a 3-hour seminar on the subject. And yes, if you're wondering, we really think it is that important.

Differentiation is the golden treasure for a retailer. In fact when you think about it, it is the magic elixir for a bank a restaurant or any other endeavor that relies on attracting participants or patrons. By differentiating you literally make your operation unforgettable.

Here's the 2-minute version of attaining differentiation. There are 6 available attributes by which you can make your business stand above its competitors and therefore make it relevant to your customers. They are: Proximity, Product, People, Presentation, Price and Promotion. We call them the 6 Ps. My guess is that you can see why.

When we refer to Proximity, we're talking about location, of course. But we're also referring to other attributes of location like, convenience of access and the amount of retail pull generated by adjacent retail centers.

Product can offer differentiation too if it is broader, deeper or unique to competitors in the area.

Our third P, People, refers to employees, their quantity, quality, training and attitudes. Funny thing is that many retailers think they own an edge with their people, but that's not always true.

Presentation refers to the environment that has been created to showcase the product offering and includes things like décor, lighting and layout.

Price is self-explanatory and for most operations low price should not be the main point of differentiation. In fact, I have written "there will only be one lowest priced operation, make sure yours is not it".

Promotion refers to how successfully the store's marketing and advertising campaign is carried out.

OK, that explains the terms. Now the challenge is to first identify the boundaries of your competitive arena and then to objectively assess at what level you compete in each category. In order of how they perform on each of these attributes, score your competitors' stores against each other and yours. When you're done, you'll have a good idea what you need to change to improve performance of your operation. Dominate the scorecard on as few as three of the attributes and the chances are high that your store will compete quite successfully. Your store will become virtually unforgettable.

You've made me so very happy.

Excerpt from Wikipedia

"You've Made Me So Very Happy" *is a song written by* [Brenda Holloway](#), [Patrice Holloway](#), [Frank Wilson](#) *and* [Berry Gordy](#), *and was released first as a single in 1967 by Holloway on the* [Tamla](#) *label. The song was later a huge hit for* [jazz-rock](#) *band* [Blood, Sweat & Tears](#) *in 1969.*

There was an article titled "Reality Check" in the October, 2009 Issue of Hardware Retailing. It was an interesting piece that underscored the alarming disconnect between hardware retailers and their customers regarding what constituted good customer service. For example when they were asked; what was the one most important element of good customer service, nearly 70% of the retailers answered "knowledgeable employees". Contrasted, just barely over 50% of consumers agreed. In fact, over 20% of consumers said instead that a wide selection of products was the one thing, while barely 5% of the retailers saw it that way. That's pretty fascinating and leads one to wonder how that type of disconnect can occur.

It could be something as simple as tradition or what we've been taught to believe. In this discussion, there are a few things we can accept as facts though. Consumers are changing. They are exposed to more products and more information, more choices and more ways to buy. With these elements at play it's important to stay in touch with what consumers are looking for. The trade rags probably offer the best insight through articles like the one I referenced earlier. Read and study. Become sponges for additional insights.

When separating your store from the others out there, it will really be to your advantage to offer more of what people are looking for. And as we've just learned that may be something completely different than what you've expected.

One thing that is hard for retailers, I think, is to separate what their needs and wants are from what their customers' needs and wants are. I believe the merchants who win are the ones who are able to recognize and offer what their customers are looking for.

If you do a search for our book, Discovery-Based Retail on the Internet, you will probably get hundreds of hits. The overwhelming amount of those hits will be referencing the definition that we gave for customer service: *Customer service is the sum of all acts and elements that allow a customer to receive what they need or desire from your retail establishment.* So how do you make your customers so very happy? Make sure that you filter your store through their eyes and perspective.

I hear you knocking.

Excerpt from Wikipedia

"I Hear You Knocking" (sometimes spelled "I Hear You Knockin'") is a <u>popular</u> <u>rhythm and blues</u> <u>song</u> with emphatic <u>syncopation</u>, written by <u>Dave Bartholomew</u> and Pearl King and published in <u>1955</u>. The original recording was made by <u>Smiley Lewis</u>, reaching #2 on the <u>Billboard R&B singles chart</u> in 1955.

I hear you knocking and in this case, you are opportunity. Opportunity knocking is one of those clichés that we hear used occasionally but as far as retail lessons go, it's a good one.

Opportunity in retail might refer to something that represents a chance to produce more sales or more profit or to expand a category, a store's footprint or maybe even open another location. Opportunity in retail means observing a void, researching the potential represented by that void, and then finally filling it in a profitable way.

We can't cover all of those opportunities in one lesson, so let's look at the expansion of a single category. An elementary example of this might be simply locating a niche within your product categories and then working to specialize in that niche. So here are suggestions of ways to go about finding that niche. Look within your own store and locate categories that you already excel in. It could be that by simply expanding that offering you create even better results by adhering to "do what you do do well". A niche, simply by the word itself, brings to mind a very narrow category. But if by expanding an offering in an already booming category you differentiate yourself then you have taken a category and made it into your niche. A wider offering within a category can do this, providing that within demographics of your retail pull area, there is sufficient demand.

But where do you find the space to expand the category when the store is already full? That is the purpose for doing an examination of the space productivity of your store. Determine each department's productivity in relationship to the space that it squanders. You will find, I am sure, departments whose productivity is not relative to the space you have devoted.

Once you determine those departments plan a way to shrink them. That might involve things as simple as closing out slow items or showing fewer facings. Whatever it takes, reclaim that space and make room for expanding the booming department. A term given to space that is not as productive as it could be is "opportunity costs".

Complete the procedure, develop your niche, minimize your opportunity costs and listen when opportunity knocks.

Love won't let me wait.

Excerpt from Wikipedia

"Love Won't Let Me Wait" *is a 1975 single by* <u>Major Harris</u>, *a former member of* <u>R&B</u>/<u>soul</u> *group* <u>The Delfonics</u>. *Written by* <u>Vinnie Barrett</u> *and* <u>Bobby Eli</u>, *the single is considered to be a staple of classic soul playlists and was Harris' only entry into the top five on both the soul and pop charts. The single hit number five on the pop chart, giving Harris a Gold record and also hit number one on the soul chart for one week.*[1]

You're store can't stock everything your customers want. In fact, no store, not even the largest widest assorted store can. It makes sense to promote special orders as part of your product offering then, doesn't it?

It seems that almost every store does special order things from time to time, but the point here is to actively promote it as part of your everyday business. Special orders will take on different attributes depending on product mix and sourcing. For example if yours is a clothing store it may be difficult to order a particular size if you drop ship directly from a manufacturer and must maintain minimum orders. But if you're sourcing through a distributor then you've got a golden paved road to capitalizing on this opportunity.

Consider developing a special area, a kiosk with catalogs, brochures or computer monitors, to encourage customers to explore additional available items. It will be necessary to develop a way to follow up with these items...e.g. a special place or special screen on your point of sale so that everyone can learn the status of special orders. Invest in some posters and other signage to decorate the area and let everyone know that you want them to explore your special offerings. Include in your communication pieces your rules and details of when the merchandise can be expected.

You won't double your store's volume with special orders. What you can do is expand the productivity of your sales space and increase your other productivity ratios. It's an easy way to increase sales without expanding inventory.

We live in an "I want it now society", don't we? Instant gratification and the proliferation of large stores with expanded inventories play into this mentality. But still, given all of that, Internet sales are increasing at a rapid rate. Those people are waiting aren't they? I believe it's just because there is yet more choice. You have at your disposal, probably literally thousands of items that you can sell that you will never stock. And although love may not let one wait, I believe your customers will wait if you start actively including special orders as part of your business model.

You ain't seen nothing yet.

Excerpt from Wikipedia

*"**You Ain't Seen Nothin' Yet**" is a <u>rock song</u> written by <u>Randy Bachman</u> and performed by <u>Bachman–Turner Overdrive</u> (BTO) on the album <u>Not Fragile</u>. It was released as a single in <u>1974</u> with an instrumental track "Free Wheelin'" as the B-side. It reached the #1 position on the Billboard Hot 100 singles chart and the Canadian <u>RPM</u> chart the week of November 9, 1974 and also reached #2 on the <u>UK Singles Chart</u>. The single won the <u>Juno Award</u> for best-selling single of 1974.*

How often are you bringing new items into your store? Of course, the answer to that question is determined in some part by your product offering. For example, if yours is a fashion store then the changing styles dictate that your stock changes, not only from season to season, but also from trend to trend. Inventory in hardware stores, on the other hand, is more static. For example, door hinges today look much like they did when I started in the business 35 years ago.

But regardless of product mix, change is necessary to maintain interest. New items come and go, or they should. But that brings us to a critical issue for many retailers; purging inventory that is not moving. I could take you into a number of stores and show you product that hasn't sold for a long time and yet, hasn't been closed out. That's a sad thing, isn't it? The slow selling merchandise takes up shelf space and inventory dollars and creates exorbitant opportunity costs. If you are one that has trouble marking down inventory to get rid of it, it's time to examine your motivation.

But here again there are some differences in product offering. In defense of hardware stores, for example, the hard to find, slow turning items may provide some of the pull that the store possesses. So how do you achieve a balance? I guess you're going to have to use some good old-fashioned common sense but remember, if you are going to inventory something for a longer time, the markup that the item commands must be higher. It makes sense, doesn't it? If the item is truly that hard to find then it definitely is not price sensitive. If it is price sensitive then we've got another problem don't we?

Kind of got off topic there didn't I? I started talking about bringing in new items and ended up talking about getting rid of old ones. But here's the deal; your available inventory dollars are finite and your display space is limited too. That means in order to bring in something new, something your customers haven't seen yet, you will need both dollars and space.

The whole point of this discussion is to encourage you to review your "dogs" report (or whatever you call it) and to formulate a strategy for selling through those items. What's that? You say you've tried? Well if you have and if you've been unsuccessful at selling them, then box those items and have them auctioned or even donate them to a civic organization. In this situation you won't recover the dollars, but you can recover the space.

One last point: in addition to the space and dollars, consider how those items lurking in your store for years affect the appearance of everything around them. Come on, cowboy up, and clean house!

Final thoughts.

Well, there you have it. We hope these short lessons help you get your sales and your crew rocking!

Watch for Volume 2 of Rock Your Retail coming soon.

In the meantime check out <u>Discovery-Based Retail</u> and <u>10 Weeks to a Better Retail Operation</u> also by Philip H. Mitchell and Gary Petz.